Patterned Threads
Ikat Traditions and Inspirations

Lotus Stack

The Minneapolis Institute of Arts

This book was produced in conjunction with the exhibition "Patterned Threads: Ikat Traditions and Inspirations," held at The Minneapolis Institute of Arts, 27 June-6 September 1987.

Designed by Anne Knauff
Edited by Leslie Reindl and Elisabeth Sövik
Photographs by Gary Mortensen

© 1987 by The Minneapolis Institute of Arts
2400 Third Avenue South
Minneapolis, Minnesota 55404
All rights reserved
Printed in the United States of America

Library of Congress Catalog Card Number 87-61330
International Standard Book Number 0-912964-33-2

This publication was funded in part by the Andrew W. Mellon Foundation.

Cover illustration:
Detail of yardage
Central Asia, 19th century
Warp ikat, cotton and silk
Gift of Ellen and Fred Wells, 86.31

Contents

Preface	4
Introduction	5
Central Asia and Persia	6
Indonesia	10
India	12
Japan	16
Mesoamerica	18
Europe	22
Patterned-Thread Techniques	26
Map	32
Appendix	34
Glossary	35
Suggested Reading	36
Exhibition Staff	37

Preface

This is the first in a series of books on the textile collection of The Minneapolis Institute of Arts. Each one will present a technique of cloth making and discuss its use by various cultures throughout history. Besides introducing the museum's textile holdings, these publications are meant to provide general information that will enable readers to appreciate other textiles they may encounter.

Patterned Threads outlines the basics of the ikat technique and describes many of the fabrics produced by this distinctive process. It is not a complete survey of all ikat cloth, but covers ikat production only in those geographical areas where pieces in the museum's collection or in some of the local private collections originated. Thus, it does not deal with ikats of Africa, the Middle East, or South America. For readers interested in pursuing the topic further, a brief bibliography is included. A summary of the museum's ikat holdings appears in the Appendix.

For their efforts in the preparation of this catalogue and exhibition I extend special thanks to Peggy Dorwick, Mary Ann Butterfield, Ainslee Beery, and Renae Malik, of the Textile Department staff; editors Leslie Reindl and Elisabeth Sövik; designers Roxy Ballard and Anne Knauff; Gwen Bitz, the museum's registrar; Gary Mortensen and Robert Fogt, photographers; R. Patrick Atherton, typesetter; and Tom Jance, Patti Landres, Doug Kroeger, John Black, Nina Chenault, Wayne Masterson, Gregg Zimmer, and Brian Stieler, exhibition technicians. Alan Shestack, Director; Timothy Fiske, Associate Director; and Michael Conforti, Chairman of the Curatorial Division, have supported this project with enthusiasm. Finally, I wish to express my gratitude to Robert Davidian, Roberta and Richard Simmons, Edward Stack, Susan and John Michelman, and Elizabeth and Lloyd Olson, whose generous loans have enhanced the exhibition immeasurably.

Introduction

Cloth woven from patterned threads has been made for at least thirteen centuries. It is thought that techniques of dyeing and weaving patterned threads originated with the various non-Chinese tribes of present-day south and southwest China and probably the northern parts of mainland Southeast Asia. From these tribal cultures the art spread northward to China and then to other regions, becoming more highly refined as diverse peoples adapted it to their own needs.

The oldest method of creating patterned threads is a technique called *ikat*. Before the thread is dyed, segments of it are tightly bound so that they will resist (i.e., not absorb) the dye, thus producing a pattern that will be fully developed when the threads are woven.

There is evidence that this technique was known and used in many areas of the world from the seventh century on. The earliest extant ikat fabric is a silk fragment housed in the Horyu-ji temple in Nara, Japan. It is dated to the later part of the Asuka period (552–644) but is generally thought to have been imported to Japan from the Asiatic mainland. Although no Indian textiles of such early date survive, some of the fabrics represented in the seventh-century cave paintings at Ajanta appear to be made of ikat cloth. There are written sources from this period that ascribe a knowledge of ikat to Yemen, in southern Arabia. And ikat textiles whose embroidered or printed inscriptions date them to the tenth or twelfth century and indicate a Yemeni provenance have been unearthed at excavations in Egypt, mostly at Fostat. Archeological finds in Peru show that the technique was also known in the Americas before the arrival of Columbus.

The ikat technique eventually became known in almost every part of the world. By the eighteenth century, cloth made of patterned threads was being worn by Uzbek nomads and Swiss peasants, and by nobles in the royal courts of France and Indonesia. The popularity of this cloth in Europe led the French, toward the end of the century, to develop a less labor-intensive means of producing patterned threads. By the 1820s, a method of printing patterns on warp threads had been refined and was a great commercial success.

The abundance and diversity of patterned-thread fabrics from the nineteenth century attest to the extensive use throughout the world of the various techniques for making such cloth. But after World War I, changes in fashion, along with altered political and economic conditions, greatly reduced ikat production.

Within the last twenty years, however, a growing interest in fine craft and ethnographic art has made patterned-thread cloth popular once again. In places where ikat never entirely disappeared it is now viewed with new respect, and in some areas it is proving profitable in the tourist trade. Textile designers, especially those working in fashion and interior design, have been using warp printing techniques to develop fabrics with the eighties look.

Some of the most exciting contemporary ikat work is being done by fiber artists in the United States and Japan. Using the traditional techniques of resist dyeing, dip dyeing, and warp painting, these artists are exploring the use of patterned threads both for practical purposes and as an art form. Their pieces include wearable art, wall hangings, and a variety of innovative textile forms.

Opposite: *Parda*
Probably Ferghana, 19th century
Warp ikat, silk and cotton
Gift of Ellen and Sheldon Sturgis, 84.29

Below: detail

Central Asia and Persia

Until the early twentieth century, Central Asia was a land of nomads and oasis populations, whose ways of life reflected different cultural and ethnic patterns. The oasis towns, where Persian influence was strong, were centers of continuing tradition. Their location at natural water sources in an otherwise arid land had encouraged intensive agricultural development, which supported a settled and stable population. The existence of a stable population was conducive to the establishment and growth of cottage industries, which tended to specialize in craft production. This pattern of development in the oases was reinforced by the geographical location of the towns, for they were on the natural trade routes of the local nomads as well as of the caravans that traveled from China to the Near East and Europe.

For centuries Central Asia was subject to Turkic and Mongolian invasions. The last major incursion resulted in the establishment of the Uzbek Empire at the beginning of the sixteenth century. By the middle of the eighteenth century this unified empire had broken up into three principal Uzbek-ruled confederations of towns and villages, called khanates, populated chiefly by descendants of the pre-Turkic tribes. The khanates were named after the leading urban centers: Khiva, Bukhara, and Kokand.

Ikat Production

The khanates of Bukhara and Kokand were famous for their ikats. These textiles were produced in the towns but were used particularly by the Uzbek population, both nomad and urban, as designators of wealth and prestige. Ikat pieces were considered valuable and were treasured by families for many generations.

Traditional ikat production techniques were used in both Central Asia and the Persian ikat centers of Kashan and Yazd. They are still used in Iran, the modern state that succeeded Persia in 1935. The process required several specialists, who sometimes worked together but more often practiced their crafts in small home workshops. In general, ikat production was carried on by men, but women were sometimes involved, especially in workshops connected with the home.

The thread used for ikat was made from locally produced cotton or silk. The cotton was spun and used as the weft. Less expensive than silk, it was employed for economic and possibly religious reasons. In Iran cotton is still used as a somewhat bulky weft for velvet ikat

mats. In some parts of the Islamic world men were (and still are) prohibited from wearing all-silk clothing. A cotton weft in a warp-faced silk fabric gave the illusion of total luxury while fulfilling the letter of the law!

Dyers who specialized in patterned threads bought thread from spinners. Within the dyeing workshop there were at least two divisions of labor: marking and wrapping of the resist on the threads, and dye preparation and coloring of the thread. The completed patterned threads were sold to local weavers, who wove them into cloth. The fabric was then purchased by tailors and other textile specialists who created wall hangings, door and bed coverings, and clothes for men, women, and children.

Throughout the area, the most popular patterned-thread fabric was a warp-dominated plain weave, although other woven structures such as satin and velvet were also used. Sometimes the mushru fabric of silk and cotton was given a special finish to stiffen it and enhance the shine. Egg white, often mixed with glue, was applied to the surface; the cloth was folded; and then the cloth was beaten with large wooden hammers.

This created a moiré effect, giving the appearance of watered silk to the surface of the fabric. Velvet made from patterned threads is quite rare. Kashan is known for its interesting velvet ikat mats, but it is the Bukhara velvet that is considered outstanding.

Some regional differences in the ikat cloth produced in Iran today and that formerly produced in Central Asia are quite apparent, whereas others are subtle. The cloth is woven much wider than it was in Central Asia, where individual panels averaged fifteen to nineteen inches wide. Also, in Iran large backgrounds are important design elements, whereas the Central Asian tradition favored extensive distribution of the motifs throughout the fabric. The differences between the fabrics from Bukhara and those from Kokand usually have to do with choice of colors and preferred combinations, as well as configurations of motifs.

Ikat Colors

The most complex of the Central Asian ikats are thought to have been produced in Ferghana, Kokand khanate, where seven colors were frequently used: yellow, wine-red, green, black, blue, violet, and of course white. The standard in Bukhara was yellow, wine-red, and pink. Certain color relationships were considered more desirable than others. In Ferghana, yellow could be adjacent to green or violet but not to white, and pink placed next to green was thought ugly. The Kokand khanate tended toward complicated, fine, multi-colored fabric, while in Bukhara larger, bolder designs were favored.

Uses of Ikat Cloth

In Central Asia most ikat cloth seems to have been made into clothing, which was one of the main expressions of wealth and dignity. The overcoat (*khalat*) was worn every day as well as on ceremonial occasions. The fashion was to wear khalats layered, the newest and finest on top. They were also exchanged on gift-giving occasions. *Chapans* (quilted overcoats), *kurtas* and *kaltachas* (tunics), and women's slacks also were made of ikat cloth.

Pardas (large, rectangular, multipurpose pieces, lined and quilted) were made of ikat fabric in Central Asia and are still being produced the same way in Iran. Though not used as extensively as they once were, they still serve the many purposes of wall or door covering, room or tent divider, and bed cover.

Future of Ikat Production

In the twentieth century, political and economic changes in this part of the world have altered ways of life, including craft techniques. The Persian ikat centers of Yazd and Kashan in present-day Iran are still using fundamentally traditional techniques, but rayon is now used more extensively than silk, and synthetic powders have replaced the traditional natural dyes. In Central Asia, now part of the Soviet Union, little traditional ikat is produced, but many of the old ikat patterns are still seen in textiles and are especially popular in Uzbekistan, where they have become a sign of national identity. Some of the textiles are warp printed, while others are imitations made with surface prints.

A few of the families that formerly made patterned threads in the Kokand khanate migrated to northern Afghanistan during the first quarter of this century and were still producing a few all-silk ikats in the early 1970s. But with the continuing political unrest and social change, it is doubtful that the tradition will survive there.

Parda, detail
Bukhara, early 20th century
Warp ikat, silk
The Ethel Morrison Van Derlip Fund, 81.49.1

Indonesia

Indonesia, a land of more than 13,000 islands extending over several thousand miles, comprises a very diverse cultural grouping. Four major religions—Islam, Christianity, Buddhism, and Hinduism—are represented here, and many tribal peoples still adhere to animistic beliefs. Even more than Central Asia, this area has been affected by waves of migrations. Scholars believe that warp ikat and the body-tension loom were first introduced into what is now Indonesia between the eighth and second centuries B.C., when migrants from the area that is now northern Vietnam and southern China first came to the archipelago. A few centuries later, extensive trade with India brought cultural influences that greatly affected artistic and craft development, especially on the islands of Java, Sumatra, and Bali. Weft ikat is thought to have been introduced in the fourteenth and fifteenth centuries by Islamic Indian and Arab traders.

Ikat Production

Cotton is indigenous to Indonesia and was the fiber preferred by the ancient peoples of the islands. It is the traditional material used for warp ikat, which is the oldest of the resist dye textile techniques used in Indonesia. Silk, which is not native to the islands, seems to have been first incorporated into the Indonesian weaving tradition toward the end of the first millennium. Weft ikat, although not unknown in cotton cloth, is more closely associated with silk.

The older, tribal cultures of Indonesia have strong craft traditions. In many of these groups, weaving became the main form of artistic expression, and the technology was handed down from one generation to the next. In areas where ancient traditions have continued well into the twentieth century, it is the women who produce the textiles. The techniques of fiber preparation, spinning, dyeing, weaving, and so on, as well as the ritual traditions and proscriptions associated with the process, are passed from mother to daughter. There is some specialization, but not in the commercial sense or to the degree seen in many other parts of the world. Often the ikat dyer (or a younger female member of her family) will also have spun the thread, and the same person may later weave the thread and sew the cloth into the finished garment or hanging. Both warp and weft ikat fabrics of exceptional quality are woven on simple body-tension looms. The village of Tenganan, on the island of Bali, produces a special ikat cloth with both the warp and the weft threads dyed so as to create an integrated double ikat cloth (*geringsing*). Indonesian ikats are made into garments and banners for religious and ceremonial use as well as other, more utilitarian, pieces.

Uses and Symbolism

Ikats often were symbols of power, prestige, and concrete riches. On many of the islands where court traditions existed, certain elaborate patterns and color combinations were reserved for royalty and the aristocracy. In areas where the exchange of gifts was an important part of ceremonial occasions, textiles represented real wealth. Some pieces made for funeral rites and to be interred with the dead naturally had a limited existence. Most ceremonial pieces, however, were used only a few times during each generation; they were carefully preserved as important heirlooms and considered part of the family wealth.

The process of creating a ceremonial textile was often as important as the care and use of the finished piece. The activities and diets of dyers and weavers working on ritual cloth were restricted, and auspicious times for beginning and continuing the work were carefully determined. For the most part, patterns were traditional, and great care was taken to produce the finest of textiles, as the quality of the fabric not only reflected on the maker's reputation but was also a link to the maker's ancestors and the supernatural world.

Production Today

Both warp and weft ikat are still being made in Indonesia today; however, the production is not as widespread as it once was, and the use of handspun thread and natural dyes is relatively rare. In the past much of the ikat was intended for either personal or ceremonial use within the weavers' culture. Today ikat is often made for the tourist trade as a source of income. Rayon is now being used in addition to cotton and silk, and some of the traditional work patterns have been altered. Workshops in which the labor is divided and specialized are now producing weft ikats on the islands of Sulawesi, Java, and Bali. Much of the ikat work is performed by young men, and the weaving is done on treadle looms with flying shuttles!

Sarong, detail
19th century
Warp ikat, cotton
Gift of Susan and John Michelman, 86.75

Sari, detail
Orissa, ca. 1980s
Weft ikat, silk
Gift of Carol Ann MacKay, 87.20.1

India

India has long been known for its rich textile tradition. Remains of Indian cloth have been found in Egyptian tombs and Japanese temples. Europe's Eastern trade of the sixteenth and seventeenth centuries depended on Indian fabrics, which in the spice-rich areas of Indonesia and Africa were considered more valuable than silver or gold. Although no early ikat Indian fabrics have been found, evidence points to a patterned-thread tradition in India of well over a thousand years.

Buddhist cave paintings done at Ajanta in the seventh century depict female servants, dancers, and musicians wearing garments that appear to be made of ikat cloth. The first known mention of *patola*, the Indian term for double ikat, is in twelfth-century documents, and trade records show that patola saris and shawls were being exported to Indonesia as early as the sixteenth century. Other records indicate that in the past ikat textiles were produced in India for the Arab world.

The most famous Indian ikats are the intricate patolas made in the state of Gujarat. The warp and weft threads are patterned in such a way that when woven, the dyed sections are aligned to form a single unified design. Nowhere else, except in the village of Tenganan on the island of Bali, are such precise and complex double ikats woven.

Patola textiles are traditionally woven by the Salvi silk-weaving community. Legend has it that this group of hereditary weavers originally lived near Hyderabad and began migrating north to Gujarat sometime in the twelfth century. They presumably brought a knowledge of ikat with them, but it was in their new home that they developed the patola specialty.

As the patola process is so labor intensive, patola saris and head shawls have always been luxury goods. Historically they have been worn by brides, though red saris also are traditional. Today, influenced by Western customs, some brides choose to wear white saris. However, the patola sari has not completely disappeared from weddings and is now frequently worn by the bride's mother or mother-in-law as a sign of her prosperity, religious feeling, and respect for tradition. On occasion, the groom will drape a folded patola sari over his shoulder.

In the past patola textiles were given as offerings to temples, where they would be used on holidays to cover special objects or to dress religious statues. At times the fabric itself, designed with auspicious symbols of flowers, leaves, elephants, and so on, was regarded as having magical powers and was used in healing rituals and in ceremonies to ward off evil.

For a number of reasons, patola production in Gujarat may soon come to an end. Today, although patola weavers are the highest paid ikat weavers in India, only two family workshops still weave this cloth. They are located in the town of Patan. The fabric has a small market because it is so costly. A high degree of specialization is required for patola production, and remuneration is not commensurate with that in other occupations. A considerable amount of time is needed to produce a finished product, and the work is hard and much of it rather monotonous.

However, as the tradition in one area appears to be ending, new ikat centers are developing in other parts of the country. Near Hyderabad, in the state of Andhra Pradesh, a simple ikat tradition has existed at least since the eighteenth century. Within the last forty years, some silk weavers of the area have begun to refine local ikat dyeing designs and processes and are making quite colorful saris and *rumals* (head shawls), which are sold in Delhi, Calcutta, Bombay, and Madras. Although the wages are poor, over 800 weavers in Andhra Pradesh work for the master weavers specializing in ikat techniques.

To the north, in the state of Orissa, where ikat technique seems to be an introduction of the twentieth century, weaving families have been specializing now for over two generations. Whereas in Andhra Pradesh there is no real local market for ikat textiles, in Orissa the homemade goods are quite popular and sell well in the local communities. The home markets, along with healthy national and burgeoning international markets, contribute to the livelihood of 6000 ikat specialists. Most weavers have their own home and loom, and some farm in addition to weaving. Some master weavers pay wages to others to weave the patterned threads, and then sell the finished cloth under their own names. However, local weaving co-ops are becoming more

Opposite: *Patola sari*
Gujarat, 19th century
Double ikat, silk
Gift of Miss Lily Place, 30.23.138

Below: detail

numerous. Here the weaver dyes the thread, weaves it, and sells the cloth to or through the co-op.

Traditionally all Indian ikat has been produced in cottage workshops in which the entire family works. Today most thread is purchased, except in some areas that specialize in tussah silk ikat cloth. In these areas, silk cocoons are purchased, and teenage girls reel the filament, giving it a slight twist. The women of the household do most of the thread preparation—winding, counting, stretching, and winding of the bobbins. The adolescent children wrap simple patterns that have been marked, often using a graph-paper guide. The men prepare the more elaborate designs, dye the threads, and prepare the threads for placement on the loom. They also usually weave the cloth. Today, especially in Orissa, some workshops are beginning to specialize in the dyeing or the weaving only.

Unlike most other areas of the world, India has an increasing number of ikat dyers and weavers. These craftspersons seem to be directing their efforts toward greater refinement of the ikat technique. The designs currently in use appear to be rearrangements of traditional motifs rather than the outcome of further artistic exploration. Nevertheless, it is encouraging that in India cottage production is succeeding and traditional occupations are surviving.

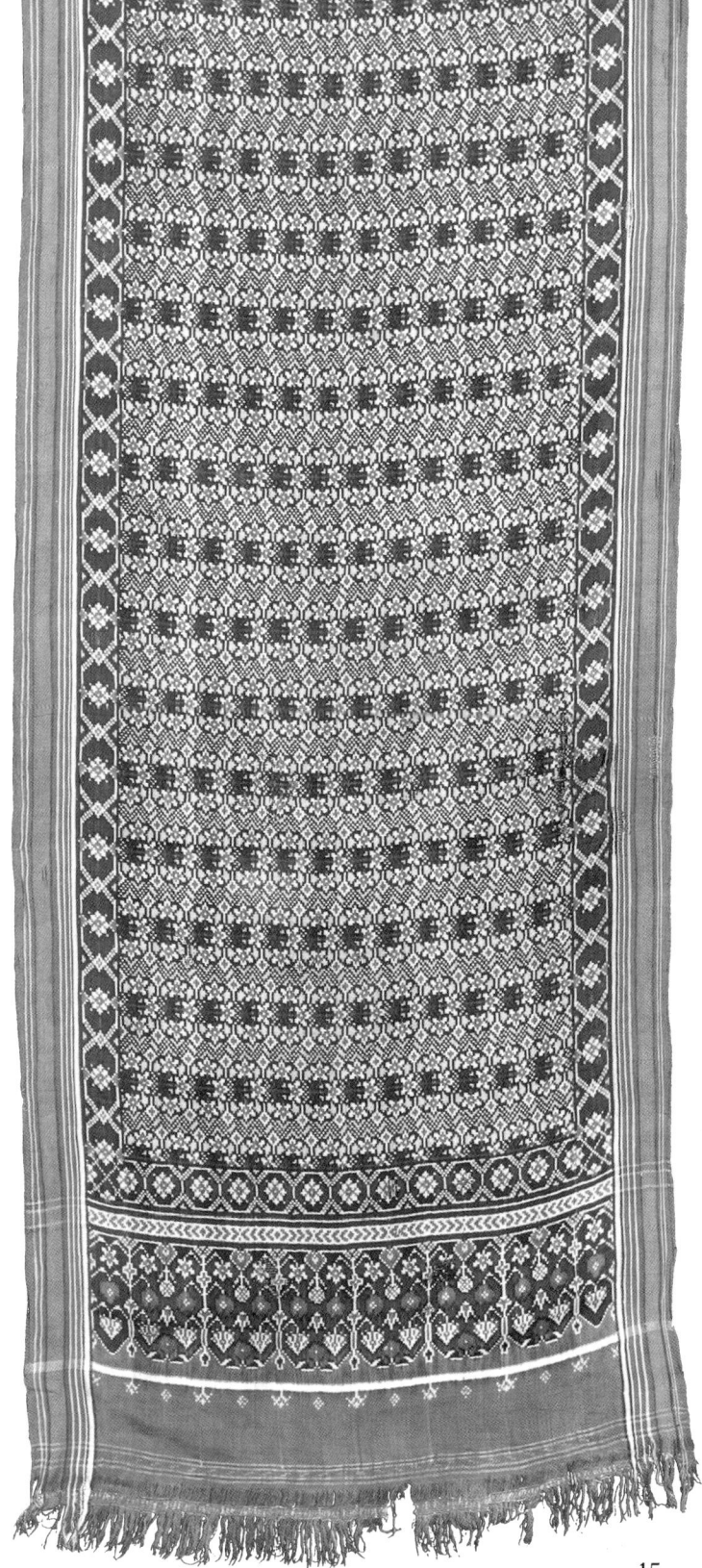

Japan

In Japan, where textile techniques are frequently named for the effect they produce rather than for the process involved, ikats are referred to as *kasuri*, possibly derived from the word *kasumi*, meaning to blur. Although the ikat process has been known in Japan for over a thousand years, it did not come into general use until the end of the seventeenth century, at which time it was mainly used to make silk fabrics for the ruling and wealthy classes. Interest in exploring the ikat tradition may have been stimulated by the arrival in Japan of the fine patterned-thread textiles made in the Ryukyu Islands. These exceptional textiles made of banana and ramie fibers were collected as taxes by the Satsuma aristocrats after the islands were added to their dominions in 1609.

Despite some interest in the early eighteenth century, the ikat technique did not really come into its own in Japan until the beginning of the nineteenth century.

Though most other ikat traditions have catered to the aristocracy, in Japan the peasant weavers developed ikat for their own use. Sumptuary laws barred peasants from wearing silk, and so they turned to readily available materials such as cotton, and used indigo, an excellent dye source. As the technique progressed, designs evolved from simple geometric patterns to more elaborate figural elements, and eventually included refined double ikats. The textiles woven on farms and in villages were used to make clothing, fabrics for interior use, and ceremonial pieces especially associated with marriage. Mothers taught their daughters how to dye and weave the wonderful blue-and-white cloth, and at the same time created part of the child's trousseau: a *futon* cover for the new home, a *furoshiki* wrapping cloth for presentation of the futon, and the special *zabuton* pillow covers. In some areas the daughters would weave ikat sashes for the bridegroom, to show their devotion and demonstrate their skill.

The Japanese developed unique adaptations to make the resist wrapping sequences for complex designs more efficient. The shifting boxes devised in Japan allowed adjustment of warp patterns after dyeing and before the threads were finally prepared for weaving. Another innovation was a procedure for painting the pile threads of velvet while weaving was in progress. The fabric created in this way retained the intense color pattern for which ikat velvets are so famous.

As time went on and ikats became more and more popular, household production alone could not meet the demand. New methods requiring extensive specialization were developed; they included *itajime kasuri* (a resist technique involving the use of carved boards) and warp printing.

Today some of the few remaining traditional ikat dyer-weavers have been designated "national treasures." Most patterned threads in Japan are mass produced in factories by the warp printing method. A few small factories specialize in the traditional resist methods and factor out the ikat thread to hand weavers; the finished cloth is then sold under the factory's name. Some ikats are produced under the auspices of community guild systems. These mini-marketing co-ops are particularly popular in Okinawa.

Most of the patterned-thread textiles produced in Japan today have traditional patterns. However, a small number of fiber artists, inspired by the old designs and natural dye colors, are doing more than just maintaining this heritage. They are building a new tradition by combining historical techniques with contemporary visual expression.

Woman's oshima tsumugu haori (short jacket), detail
First third 20th century
Double ikat, silk
Gift of Mrs. Woodbury E. Andrews, 84.47.1

Mesoamerica

Due to unfavorable conditions, archeological textile remains are almost nonexistent in Mesoamerica. Therefore it is impossible to determine from physical evidence how long ikat fabrics have been produced in this part of the world. However, circumstantial evidence strongly indicates that ikat predates the Spanish conquest. Warp and weft ikats found in ancient Peruvian grave sites establish that knowledge of the ikat process existed in the Americas before contact with Europe. Also, in the Americas, weft ikat threads, thought to be a later development than warp ikat threads, are woven on the indigenous body-tension loom. Ritual textiles are created in this way, as well as traditional clothing.

Guatemala

It is probably safe to say that today ikat clothing is worn more in Guatemala than in any other country in the world. The native population wears it for both everyday and ceremonial occasions. The skirts, slacks, blouses and shirts, belts, carrying cloths, and so on identify the wearer as belonging to a specific ethnic group, living in a particular region of Guatemala. Ikat production is of two types: that made for sale and that made for domestic use.

There are several important dyeing centers in highland Guatemala, the largest being in the departments of Quezaltenango and Totonicapán. The most famous town within this area is Salcajá. Certain families have traditionally been professional dyers, with men performing most of the work and women occasionally doing the resist wrapping. Usually the dyers only create the patterned threads and do not weave the cloth. Both warp and weft threads are dyed with traditional patterns, such as "the lyre," "the doll," "the jar," and "the small fish." Complex color combinations are not used on the individual threads themselves. The most typical color combination is blue-black and white, although some other color is often substituted for the white. Quite colorful and intricate designs result from combining various colored sets of traditional ikat patterned threads as well as from using both warp and weft ikat in the same fabric. In certain fabrics, solid strips or bands of color are incorporated into the design.

The professional dyers generally sell their patterned threads directly to professional weavers or to dry goods stores, which, in a town like Salcajá, are located around the square where the local markets are held. The professional weavers still use the foot loom introduced by the Spaniards at the time of the conquest. Traditionally this loom is operated by men, but because many workshops are in a household enclave, women also weave, and children sometimes prepare and align the ikat threads for proper placement on the loom. As alignment requires a considerable amount of space, it is often done just outside the weaving workshop in whatever space is available, be it courtyard, street, or shoulder of the highway.

The professional weaver's main product is the *corte*, or woman's skirt. In major dyeing centers in which weavers are also located, such as Salcajá in Quezaltenango and San Cristóbal and San Miguel in Totonicapán, cortes are made with traditional regional patterns and are shipped to local markets in the appropriate regions.

A weaver who weaves for her own family or locality usually purchases the ikat threads from the local market or, if in a larger town, at a dry goods store. She selects the threads in pattern sets according to traditional constraints or her own fancy. Using a body-tension loom, she weaves fabric for men's and women's clothing, carrying cloths, and elaborate shawls. The thread most often is cotton, but silk is also used; wool ikat threads are most uncommon. Weft patterned threads are generally used on body-tension looms; it is very unusual to employ both warp and weft patterned threads in the same fabric on this loom.

In a number of areas in highland Guatemala, craftspersons in cottage workshops both dye the ikat threads and weave the cloth. They provide for their own needs and also sell some of their work in the local markets.

Perraje, detail
Guatemala, ca. 1940s
Weft ikat, cotton
Gift of Elizabeth and Lloyd Olson, 86.98.9

Rebozo
Guatemala, ca. 1940s
Shifted warp ikat, silk and cotton
Gift of Elizabeth and Lloyd Olson, 86.98.7

Again, ikat fabrics are labor intensive and their production takes time. The very finest are expensive and considered luxury goods, although it should be kept in mind that a set of fine clothes is regarded as a necessity by many people throughout the world. In Guatemala the quality of ikat fabric can vary greatly. The complexity of the design, the amount of ikat thread in the textile, the alignment of the patterned threads, the type of yarn (cotton or silk), and the excellence of the weaving all affect the price charged for the cloth. As long as ethnic identity is associated with ikat cloth and the economic base of the country remains relatively stable, it seems likely that resist-dyed patterned threads will continue to be widely used in Guatemala.

Mexico

The other area of Mesoamerica in which ikat is still produced is Mexico. Santa María del Río, known for its work with silk and rayon, and Tenancingo, known for fine cotton fabrics, are the most famous centers. Both towns produce refined *rebozos* with delicate warp ikat patterns and elaborate tied fringes. The threads are woven on either body-tension looms or foot looms. These shawls are worn in Mexico by Indian women and mestizas alike.

As in Guatemala, it is difficult to determine whether the ikat tradition was introduced with the Spanish invasion or predated the conquest. We do know that as recently as the 1930s it was closely associated with certain Indian groups in Mexico, primarily the Otomi weavers from Tolimán in the state of Querétaro and from Ixmiquilpan and Zimapán in the state of Hidalgo. In the past both warp and weft ikat were produced, and more elaborate patterns were incorporated into the design than those now used. The work done today is precise and well crafted, but the design variations are rather limited.

Corte (woman's skirt), detail
Guatemala, first quarter 20th century
Weft ikat, rayon and cotton
Gift of Mrs. Stanley Hawks, 78.19.13

Chiné panel, detail
Lyon, France, 20th century
Warp printed, silk
The Christina N. and Swan J. Turnblad Memorial Fund, 81.93.12

Europe

Europe appears to have been exposed to ikat initially in the tenth century, through Arab settlements in Sicily and Spain. The Arabs themselves had become familiar with the technique through their contacts with India. In ikat fabrics produced in Yemen during the ninth century, which have been found in Egyptian burial grounds, the motifs and arrangements of motifs are markedly similar to those seen in the cloth later woven in Italy and Majorca. This Eastern influence was later reinforced, for from the Renaissance onward Italy had close commercial ties with the Ottoman Empire, and not only finished textiles but also information on technique and style were exchanged.

From the beginning of the Renaissance through the seventeenth century, Italy exported many textiles to the rest of Europe and thus greatly influenced styles and techniques in other production centers. The ikat textiles of this period were used mainly for upholstery and wall hangings, although a number were designed for ecclesiastical purposes. The motifs were for the most part geometric, with arrowhead and lozenge patterns, often arranged between plain bands, being especially popular. Warp ikat was the dominant form for these fabrics.

By the eighteenth century the ikat technique was in use throughout most of Europe, and the styles expressed regional preferences. In Scandinavia, where wool was abundant and much of the textile production was done in the home, weft ikat was favored for bed coverings and for skirts and jackets. On some of the small islands near Sweden and Denmark, fishermen's hats were knitted from patterned threads. (This is one of the few places in the world where ikat threads were used in nonwoven forms.) In Germany and Switzerland, silk shawls were produced that contained both warp and weft ikat threads. These shawls were so popular in some parts of Switzerland that they were incorporated into the regional costume.

Perhaps the area to be influenced by Italian ikats earliest was the island of Majorca. Majorca is now the only place in Europe where ikat fabric is still produced. In the farmhouses near the town of Pollensa, many cotton blankets, door curtains, and chair upholsteries are still being made by craftsmen who learned the art from their fathers. The traditional blue-and-white arrowhead pattern, called *tela de lenguas*, is still very popular.

By far the best known European ikats are those made in France. During the seventeenth century, under the guidance of Louis XIV's minister of commerce, Jean-Baptiste Colbert, France took the lead from Italy and became the major textile producer and exporter in Europe. Although in Lyon, the silk capital of France, ikat fabrics inspired by Italian designs had been made since the sixteenth century, the famous *chiné à la branche* fabrics didn't come into their own until the late seventeenth century. In developing these lovely floral ikat fabrics, French designers and craftsmen were influenced by the elaborate and intricate ikats worn by the Siamese envoys visiting the French court in 1684. During the reigns of Louis XV, Louis XVI, and Napoleon, *chiné à la branche* silks from Lyon were used in palaces to cover walls and upholster furniture, and made into clothing for men and women of the court. Depending on the intended use, ikat fabrics were woven as simple plain weaves or as complex satins or velvets.

In addition to the resist dye technique employed at this time in many of the French textile centers, other ways to create patterned threads were being developed by textile artists. The most successful was Gaspard Grégoire (1751–1846), who received a patent for his technique of warp painting in 1788. Grégoire's extremely detailed and delicate warp-painted velvet pictures included portraits of the aristocracy, mythological figures, and images of flowers and birds. None of his many imitators has succeeded in duplicating the subtlety of his work.

At this time great strides were being made in textile printing technology. Because ikat production was so labor intensive, attempts were made to achieve the same effect more economically, by means of printing. In 1816 a warp printing process was patented and proved so efficient that it was soon adopted in many European textile centers. Warp-printed fabrics were very popular during the nineteenth century in Europe and America; they were used especially for ladies' dresses and for clothing accessories such as scarves, shawls, and ribbons.

Chiné panel, detail
Lyon, France, 20th century
Warp printed, silk
The Christina N. and Swan J. Turnblad Memorial Fund, 81.93.3

Steppeflower, detail
Jack Lenor Larsen, American (b. 1927)
Warp printed and jacquard woven in Switzerland
Cotton with chintz finish
Gift of the artist, 87.18

Besides the plain-weave, satin, and velvet fabrics traditionally woven with ikat threads, complex woven structures were explored in the nineteenth century. The invention of the jacquard loom had facilitated complex weave patterning, and use of this loom was combined at times with the new patterned threads to create even more elaborate and exciting designs. The French developed a new pile structure called *velours au sabre*, a name that referred to the cutting of the floating satin warp-printed threads in the patterned areas of the fabric. Many remnants of these *velours au sabre* and warp-printed textiles are seen in the American crazy quilts of the late nineteenth century.

Warp-printed fabrics went somewhat out of fashion after World War I. During the last decade, however, several European countries have increased their production, and the fabric is again being used for upholstery and fine clothing.

Patterned-Thread Techniques

Patterning of fabrics is usually done during the weaving process by arrangement of colored threads or by structural manipulation of the threads. Sometimes patterning is done after weaving, in which case the fabric is embellished with embroidery or other forms of stitching or is printed. Infrequently patterning is created even before the cloth is woven, by means of multicolored threads. The threads can be the simple variegated ones available in many knitting and sewing stores today or they can be specifically colored to create elaborate and intricate motifs. Coloring can be achieved by several different techniques. The oldest are the resist dyeing procedures, in which some form of resist is applied directly to the threads. The "newer" processes, those developed in the last 300 years, include warp painting, stenciling, and printing. Once patterned threads are created they can be woven on any type of loom. The most popular structure is plain weave, which gives a reversible fabric. However, twills, damasks, velvets, and complicated jacquard weave structures are also used.

Resist Dye Techniques

For centuries the most popular method of creating patterned threads was the resist dye technique commonly known today as *ikat*. The term *ikat* is a derivative of the Malay-Indonesian word *mengikate*, meaning to tie or to bind. In the ikat process, sections of threads are tied or bound so tightly and in such a way that they will resist absorbing color when the yarn is immersed in a dye bath. Thus, only the unbound sections of the yarn become colored. The threads are untied and retied for each dye bath of a different color. Thus, a single thread may contain several sections of different colors.

Although the ikat process has many variations throughout the world, several features are essential to it.

The threads must be under a consistent tension while the resist is being applied, to ensure evenness of the desired pattern. This necessitates the use of a tying frame, which can be as simple as the ground-staked version used in Indonesia or as elaborate as the rotating models used in some parts of France and Central Asia. The threads intended for patterning are carefully arranged on these frames so that when the

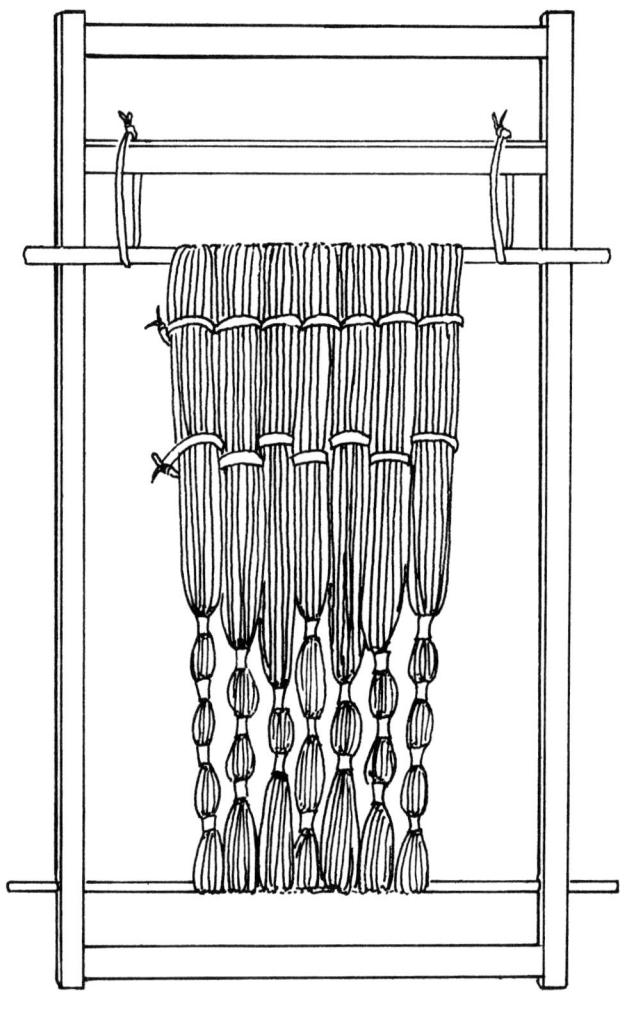

A tying frame maintains even tension on the threads while they are grouped and then wrapped according to a predetermined pattern. The wrapped segments resist absorption of dye.

tying and dyeing process is completed they can be placed on the loom ready to be woven into fabric.

The threads must be marked as to which areas are to be tied and which areas are to be free to absorb the dye. Marking is usually done by a very experienced person. In certain parts of India and Indonesia, the tying sequence is a matter of memory alone; in other parts of these countries graph-paper records or a previously woven fabric with the desired design acts as a guide for marking. In some places in Japan, stencils are used to mark a master or "mother thread" (*tane-ito*), which is then incorporated into the group of threads intended for dyeing to serve as the tying guide. In Tenancingo, Mexico, where relatively small motifs are used, the threads are stamped to indicate where the resist should be placed.

Ikat is by far the most common form of resist treatment. The few known nonwrapping resist processes include the application of wax to threads, a technique used by the tribal peoples of Hainan and by people in south and southwest China, bordering Southeast Asia. During the 1830s in Yamato, near Nara, Japan, yet another form of resist dyeing developed. This technique was an adaptation of an already existing process used to create an imitation tie-dyed fabric. In the new technique, carefully aligned threads are placed between pairs of boards carved with an identical pattern. These boards are bolted together so that certain areas of the encased threads are subjected to extreme pressure. The bolted units are then submerged in a dye bath. The recessed sections of the carved boards act as channels for the liquid dye, and the areas of threads in these recessed sectors receive the color. Although carving of the boards requires time, the boards can be reused many times and thus prove very efficient for production of patterned threads.

Wrapping Systems

The ikat technique is labor intensive and time consuming. To maximize production, various cultures have developed "shortcuts." For instance, in India, where the technique is widely used, some very efficient wrapping systems have evolved. In the state of Gujarat, intricate and complex ikats are produced to make the famous *patola* saris worn by wealthy brides and then treasured as heirlooms. The time needed to wrap the threads has been reduced by wrapping repeated patterns at one time. The threads intended for three saris are layered and then folded in half, establishing a unit of six levels, one on top of the other. Then three of these units are combined and wrapped to form a specific design segment. Thus one tying can produce the threads needed for eighteen finished design motifs. When precise patterns are desired, a combination of more than three units is not practical—if the group of threads to be tied is too bulky, it is impossible to achieve a tight, even binding that will resist absorption of color at the ends of the wrapped section.

The materials used for wrapping the yarn vary according to what is locally available. In parts of Indonesia, *agel* fiber is traditionally used; in West Africa raffia is the preferred material. In Uzbekistan and Afghanistan, where bold patterns are usual, strips of cotton cloth are employed. In Europe, parchment and later sturdy paper were tied in place with cotton yarn. The twentieth century has seen the introduction of new wrapping material. On the island of Majorca, one of the oldest European ikat centers, paper wrapping has given way to rubberbands; in Japan, nonadhesive plastic tying tape is used; and in the United States some ikat dyer-weavers use balloons!

In Central Asia, where warp design units are also wrapped in two or more groups, a cord to prevent slippage is secured at the point where the threads are folded. The cord acts as a resist, and a horizontal undyed white line will appear in the completed pattern. The line itself is often used as an alignment guide when the threads are placed on the loom. This system of resist wrapping and dyeing results in mirror-image designs flanking the white line.

Dyeing

The creation of multicolored patterned threads requires immersion of the threads in several different dye baths. There are at least two traditional basic sequences for the dye baths.

In most parts of Central Asia, where bright, clear, intense colors are preferred, the threads are dyed first with light and then with darker colors and are placed last in a light dye bath. In Bukhara, for instance, a dyeing sequence might be as follows: All sections of the thread that will

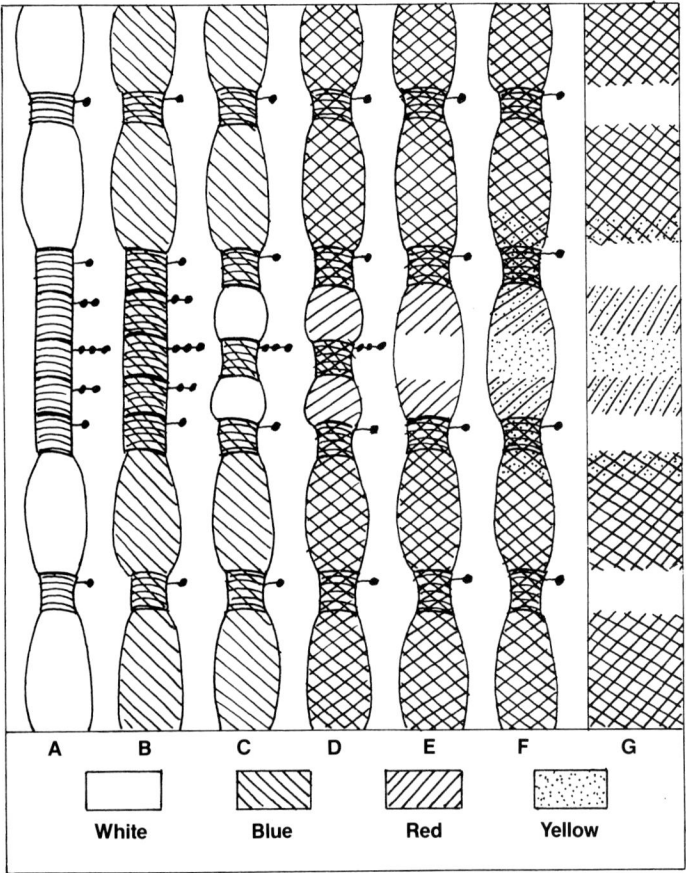

Dyeing sequence common in Indonesia: *(A)* Threads bound with knot-coded resist wrapping, ready for immersion in the blue dye bath. *(B)* Threads after removal from the blue dye bath. *(C)* The resist wrapping has been removed in two areas, and the threads are ready for the red dye bath. *(D)* Threads after removal from the red dye bath. The blue areas, which were not wrapped, have been overdyed with red and are now a dark blue-red. *(E)* More of the resist wrapping has been removed. At this point, the exposed area may simply be dipped into the next dye bath. *(F)* Threads after dip dyeing in yellow dye. Part of the blue-red area on each side of the resist has been overdyed with yellow, as well as the intentionally exposed red and white threads. The yellow dye, however, has little effect on the darker colors. *(G)* With all resist wrappings removed, the patterned threads are ready to be prepared for weaving.

remain white or eventually be dyed pink are tightly wrapped with strips of cotton cloth. The threads are then immersed in a yellow dye bath. When dyeing is completed and the threads are dry, all areas that are to remain yellow are resist wrapped to prevent absorption of red in the red dye bath. After another round of selective wrapping to preserve the red color, a green dye bath is used. Before final dyeing, all wrapping is removed except for that around sections that are to remain white. The threads are quickly dipped several times into a boiling pink dye bath, which has a minimal effect on previously dyed areas. Besides the obvious white, yellow, red, green, and pink colors that develop on the thread through this dyeing process, other colors may be introduced through overdyeing. For example, brown may be created by allowing red sections to absorb green dye.

In many places in Indonesia, where dark, rich colors are preferred, the dye bath sequence is almost reversed. The first dye bath is blue, and therefore all areas meant to be a color other than blue are resist wrapped. Light shades of blue are obtained by removing the wrapping from selected areas at some point during the blue dyeing process, as the length of time the thread is in the dye bath affects the intensity of the color. After the threads have turned the desired blue, they are dried. On the few occasions when this clear blue is to be retained, additional wrapping is tied in place. The more usual procedure, however, is simply to remove the resist wrapping in areas where the design calls for a red color. After the red dye treatment, all wrapping is removed. With the use of overdyeing and with selective removal of resist wrapping part way through a particular color process, this two-dye-bath dyeing sequence can produce a thread patterned with five colors: white, dark blue, light blue, red, and purple-black.

As noted, for the most part all wrapping is done before any dyeing begins. In some areas of Indonesia, to facilitate efficient removal of the resist wrapping in preparation for the next dye bath, the ends of the wrapping material are coded with knots that indicate which wrappings should be removed before the thread is introduced into a specific dye bath. For instance, two knots indicate that the wrapper should be removed when the red dye is to be used, whereas three knots indicate removal before exposure to the yellow dye.

In modern Japan, where nonadhesive plastic tape is frequently used for resist wrapping, coding for a specific dye bath is also used in some workshops. However, instead of knots, colored tapes communicate the needed information.

Creation of Color for Dye Baths

The creation of color, be it for fiber, thread, or fabric, is a major undertaking. Historically it involved the growing, gathering, or purchase of particular plant materials that yield specific colors. Some of the more familiar plants include indigo (blues), madder root (reds), sumac and pomegranate (yellows), and walnuts (brown). Which plants were used tended to depend on local availability. After processing, the dye material was added to a bath composed of water and substances such as tin or alum that helped make the color permanent. Days and sometimes even months were needed to obtain a desired color.

Coloring became much simpler and faster after the middle of the nineteenth century, with the development in England of synthetic dyes. The new technology spread quickly, and by the beginning of the twentieth century it was being used in most production centers around the world. By the 1950s the traditional techniques had almost all disappeared except in some remote rural areas. In the last twenty years, however, interest in natural dyes has revived, and some communities in Japan, the Near East, Mesoamerica, and Africa are once gain using local, age-old procedures to prepare colors for textiles.

Composition of Patterns

The patterned threads created to produce intricate compositions are usually designed in such a manner that only minor adjustments to refine alignment are needed before they are placed on the loom. However, certain motifs, such as the arrowhead and flame patterns, are more easily produced with simple band-dyed threads that are pulled or displaced to achieve the desired composition. This basic technique is used in many parts of the world. In Japan, special equipment is used to exploit its potential.

In ikat, the pattern commonly is applied to only one set of the weaving threads, either the warp or the weft. It is not necessary for all the threads in an ikat fabric to be patterned. Sometimes solid-color threads are placed between groups of patterned threads to form plain stripes or bands.

The warp threads for this rebozo were resist dyed in a pattern of alternating black and white horizontal bands. When placed on the loom, the threads were shifted, displacing the original pattern of bands to create a diagonal design.

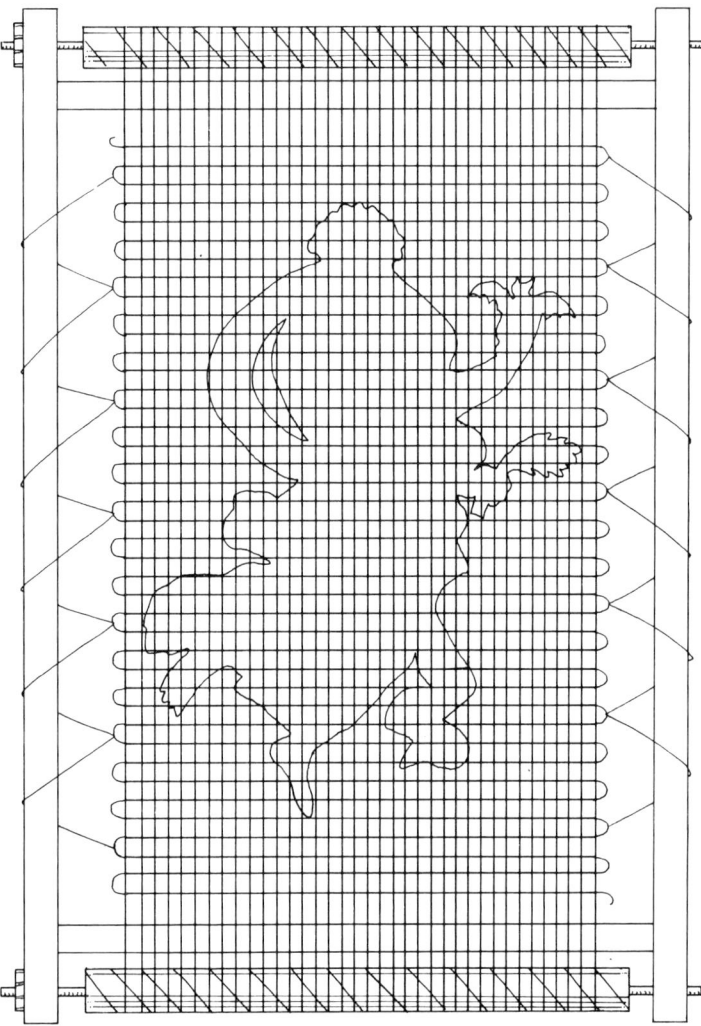

Warp painting can be used to create very intricate patterns. A few temporary weft threads are introduced to stabilize the alignment of the warp, and this "flimsy fabric" is placed on a frame, with tension on all four sides. The painter can then proceed without undue concern for maintaining the warp sequence.

Other Techniques

Although resist dyeing is probably the oldest and most widely used method of producing patterned threads, it is by no means the only method.

Dip Dyeing

One relatively simple method used to create threads with larger blocks of color than are usually associated with resist dying techniques is that of dip dyeing. It involves partial immersion of skeins of thread in a dye bath. Because nothing prevents the dye from wicking, rather imprecise bands of color develop. Threads colored in this way are often incorporated into elaborate weavings to create subtle color changes.

A modified form of dip dyeing was used in European shawl manufacturing of the nineteenth century to produce multicolored fringes and intense central patterns. The technique is still employed today in India for the threads used to weave certain styles of saris.

Warp Painting and Stenciling

Warp painting and stenciling are other methods of making patterned threads. They can be accomplished in two ways. One way is to use a loom that is ready for weaving with the warp threads in place. An inch or two of cloth is woven to align the threads perfectly. The normal weaving tension on the warp is then released, which allows these threads to be drawn out from the loom. While the original alignment is maintained, the threads are carefully placed on a rigid, padded surface and a firm tension is reestablished. Specially prepared dyes that are thicker than those normally used for dyeing are applied freehand or with the aid of stencils, depending on the design requirements. Great care must be taken not to disturb the sequence of the threads and to make sure the dye fully penetrates the area being colored.

For particularly intricate or subtle designs, the procedure is modified somewhat. A few temporary weft threads are introduced to stabilize the warp alignment, creating a "flimsy fabric." This "fabric" is removed from the loom and put in a frame, and tension is placed on all four sides. This ensures stability of the warp, freeing the painter from concern about maintaining the warp sequence. After the painting has been completed, the "fabric" is placed back on the loom, the temporary weft is removed, and a true patterned-thread textile is woven. As can be imagined, this last method is extremely labor intensive and time consuming. The first technique described, the extended warp, is used by a number of contemporary fiber artists. The second technique, the "flimsy fabric," is no longer used. Its most famous proponent was Gaspard Grégoire (1751–1846), who refined the technique to create exquisite velvets.

Warp Printing

During the nineteenth century both Europe and Japan developed new techniques to create patterned threads. In France in 1816, a patent was issued for a warp printing process that achieved a balance between the advantages of the multicolored thread process and the speed of the newly mechanized printing process. The technique as used today is similar to the warp painting process just described, as it involves a double-weaving procedure. A dense warp set is woven with a sparsely spaced, temporary weft. Resting on a well-padded surface, this "flimsy fabric" can be printed with blocks, rollers, screens, or any other properly adapted means. After the printing is completed and the threads are dry, the "fabric" is put back on the loom. The temporary weft is removed during the reweaving.

The color pattern in these warp-printed fabrics is an inherent part of the thread itself and is not simply applied to the surface of the cloth, as in normal printing. As a result, the colors in textiles woven with these (or with any other) patterned threads are often very intense; depending on the weave, the material may be reversible. In fact, during the last 200 years printed imitations have frequently been made incorporating the somewhat diffuse quality of design elements that is due to the slight shift of the patterned threads. These imitations are easily detected, because the pattern shift does not follow the structure of the fabric and because the design is present only on the face of the cloth and not on the reverse.

Warp-printed textiles and ribbons were very popular during the last half of the nineteenth century. Specialized interior and clothing fabrics are still being produced by this method in France, Switzerland, the USSR (Uzbekistan), and Japan.

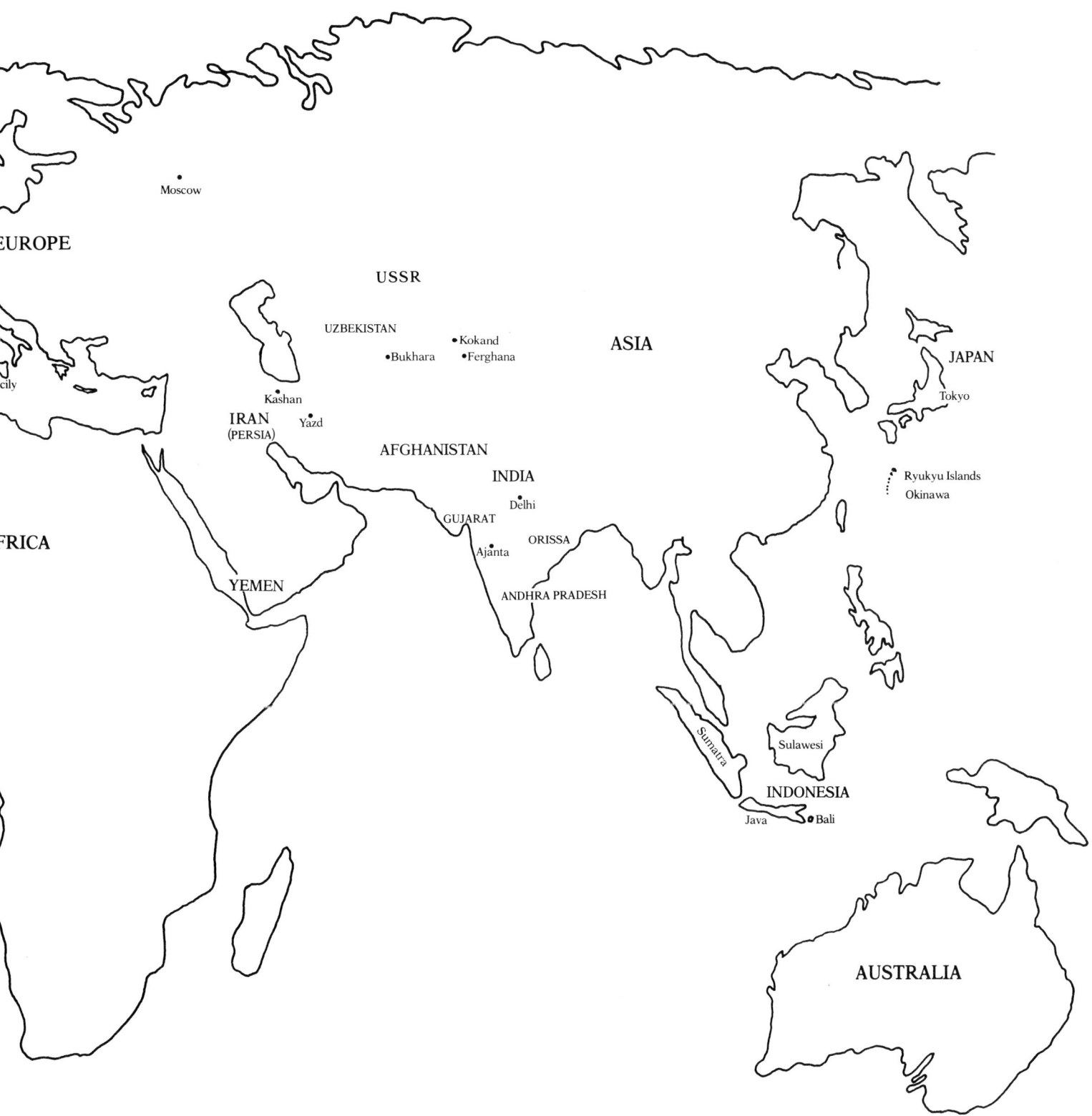

Appendix: The Ikat Collection of The Minneapolis Institute of Arts

Textiles woven from patterned threads have been acquired by the museum during three different periods. A number of Central Asian and Persian pieces were a gift of Miss Lily Place, who purchased them in the late teens and early twenties while living in Egypt. Much of the Guatemalan material came to the museum in the mid-seventies but was collected by the donor, Mrs. Stanley Hawks, in the late twenties while she was residing in Guatemala. The greatest growth has taken place during the 1980s, with the museum both purchasing and actively soliciting donations of ikat work. The collection is still in its formative stage, and future acquisitions will further develop specific cultural groupings as well as add examples of the technical variations that can be created with patterned threads.

Central Asia and Persia
There are three late nineteenth- or early twentieth-century Persian pieces: two Kashan velvets and a large Yazd silk panel. The Central Asian holdings, including a few pieces undoubtedly made in Afghanistan, comprise four pardas, a man's coat, a tunic, and thirteen loom-width panels ranging in length from twenty inches to fourteen feet. These cotton/silk and all-silk fabrics represent a variety of patterns and surface finishes used in this part of the world. There are also a number of pardas and coats in local private collections.

Indonesia
At this time the museum has only one sarong, made on the island of Flores. Several private collectors in the community own some fine pieces.

India
The museum's one Moghul textile is a silk/cotton satin-weave mushru ikat originally intended for use as a lining fabric. Other Indian ikats are a nineteenth-century patola and some costume pieces made with space-dyed threads to enhance the decorative woven pattern. Several contemporary saris made in Orissa were recently added to the collection.

Japan
There are four twentieth-century double-ikat costume pieces in the holdings of the Department of Asian Art. Local private collections contain a number of other examples.

Mesoamerica
The museum's Guatemalan ikat consists of twentieth-century costume pieces, including three women's skirts (rayon/cotton and all cotton), several shawls, and some simple belts. There are several local collectors of Guatemalan material, one of whom recently purchased a fine nineteenth-century Mapuche ikat pancho made in Chile.

Europe
There are three eighteenth-century pieces: a Grégoire warp-painted velvet; a three-colored wool velvet, probably made in Flanders; and a five-panel Italian silk satin-woven hanging. The nineteenth- and twentieth-century holdings of approximately twenty pieces are a selection of silk warp-printed ribbons and dress fabrics, most of them originally purchased in Lyon, France.

Contemporary
At present the collection contains only one ikat hanging and one warp-printed panel as contemporary artistic expressions of the patterned-thread technique. The department is acquiring contemporary textiles, so very likely more ikat pieces will be added to the museum's holdings.

Glossary

Agel fiber: Fiber of palm leaves, similar to raffia.

Corte: Skirt worn by Guatemalan Indian women.

Ikat: An Indonesian term for the process by which a pattern is resist-dyed on the warp or the weft or both before weaving begins. Widely used today for cloth made from patterned threads.

Jacquard loom: A loom with a special attachment that controls the weaving sequence by means of punched cards.

Jacquard weave: Fabric structure woven on a jacquard loom; by implication a complex structure.

Loom: A device on which cloth is woven. It stretches the warp and has a mechanism that creates an opening, or shed, for the weft to pass through.

Overdyeing: Dyeing an already colored thread with another color to make a third color. For instance, overdyeing blue thread with yellow produces green thread.

Parda: A large rectangular textile, generally lined and quilted, from Central Asia or Persia; used as a wall or door covering, room or tent divider, or bed cover.

Plain weave: A weave structure based on a unit of two warps and two wefts, in which each warp passes over one and under one weft.

Raffia: Fiber from the raffia palm.

Ramie: Fiber from the ramie plant, a member of the nettle family.

Rebozo: A shawl worn in Mexico and Guatemala.

Resist: Any material placed on or wrapped around threads to prevent the absorption of dye.

Resist dyeing: Dyeing thread or cloth that has been selectively covered with a resist material to prevent dye absorption in certain areas.

Thread: See *Yarn*.

Tussah: A type of wild silk.

Warp: The parallel threads that run longitudinally on a loom or in a fabric.

Warp set: The number of warp threads in a given unit of measure.

Weft: The transverse threads in a fabric, which are interworked with the warp.

Wicking: The migration of color, by capillary action, into dry sections of thread that is being dyed. Wicking may be desired as part of the design, or it may occur accidentally, as when a resist wrapping has not been applied properly.

Yarn: In the strictest sense, "yarn" refers to fibers or filaments used for weaving and knitting, "thread" to those used for sewing. In common usage, however, "yarn" is understood to be softly spun and employed primarily for knitting, whereas "thread" is more tightly spun and employed for fine textile work (sewing, weaving, lace making, etc.). In this publication, the terms are used interchangeably.

The following are terms used in various regions of the world for techniques of resist-dyeing and for cloth made from resist-dyed threads. A translation of the root word has been given when it could be determined.

alejah, "variegated," a Turkic word; India and Persia.

abr, "cloud," especially as reflected in water; Central Asia.

abreshahi, a Persian word; Central Asia.

bandha, "to bind"; India (Orissa).

chiné à la branche, a French term indicating the assumed Chinese origin of the technique; Europe.

chitka; India (Andhra Pradesh).

dara'i, "to bind," "to wind around"; Persia.

flammé, "flame"; a French word; Europe.

ipekshahi, a Turkic word; Central Asia.

jaspe, "lightning"; Mesoamerica.

kasuri, "blur," "mist"; Japan.

pagdu bandhu, "to bind"; India (Andhra Pradesh).

patola, refers to a special double ikat process; India (Gujarat).

tela de linguas, "tongue of flame"; Spain.

Suggested Reading

General

Bühler, Alfred. *Ikat, Batik, Plangi.* 3 vols. Basel: Pharos-Verlag Hansrudolf Schwabe, 1972. (Text in German, well illustrated)

Larsen, Jack Lenor, with Alfred Bühler, Bronwen Solyom, and Garrett Solyom. *The Dyers Art: Ikat, Batik, Plangi.* New York: Van Nostrand Reinhold, 1976.

Central Asia

Gluck, Jay, and Sumi Hiramoto Gluck, editors. *A Survey of Persian Handicraft: A Pictorial Introduction to the Contemporary Folk Arts and Art Crafts of Modern Iran.* Tehran: The Bank Melli Iran, 1977.

Klimburg, Max, and Sandra Pinto. *Tessuti ikat dell'Asia Centrale di collezioni italiane.* Turin: Umberto Allemandi & C., 1986. (Text in Italian and English)

Indonesia

Iklé, Charles F. "Ikat Technique and Dutch East Indian Ikats." *Bulletin of the Needle and Bobbin Club* 15, no. 1-2 (1931): 2-59.

Warming, Wanda, and Michael Gaworski. *The World of Indonesian Textiles.* Tokyo, New York, and San Francisco: Kodansha International, 1981.

India

Bühler, Alfred, and Eberhard Fischer. *The Patola of Gujarat: Double Ikat in India.* 2 vols. Basel: Krebs, 1979.

Bühler, Alfred, Eberhard Fischer, and Marie-Louise Nabholz. *Indian Tie-Dyed Fabrics.* Historic Textiles of India at the Calico Museum, Ahmedabad, vol. 4. Ahmedabad, India: B. U. Balsari, on behalf of Calico Museum of Textiles, 1980.

Mohanty, Bijoy Chandra, and Kalyan Krishna. *Ikat Fabrics of Orissa and Andhra Pradesh.* Study of Contemporary Textile Crafts of India, edited by Moti Chandra, vol. 1. Ahmedabad, India: Calico Museum of Textiles, 1974.

Japan

Langewis, Jaap. "Japanese Ikat Weefsels." Reprinted from *Kultuurpatronen* (Bulletin of the Ethnographical Museum in Delft) 5-6 (1963): 41-83. (Text in Dutch and English)

Tomita, Jun, and Noriko Tomita. *Japanese Ikat Weaving: The Techniques of Kasuri.* London: Routledge and Kegan Paul, 1982.

Mesoamerica

Hidalgo, Italo Morales. *La situación del jaspe en Guatemala.* Sub-Centro Regional de Artesanías y Artes Populares, Colección Tierra Adentro 4. Guatemala City, 1984. (Text in Spanish)

Osborne, Lilly de Jongh. *Indian Crafts of Guatemala and El Salvador.* Norman: University of Oklahoma Press, 1965.

Europe

Algoud, Henri. *Gaspard Grégoire et ses velours d'art.* Paris: Société Française d'Imprimerie et de Librairie, 1908. (Text in French)

Nabholz-Kartaschoff, Marie-Louise. *Ikatgewebe aus Nord- und Südeuropa.* Basler Beiträge zur Ethnologie, vol. 6. Basel: Pharos-Verlag Hansrudolf Schwabe, 1969. (Text in German)

Nabholz-Kartaschoff, Marie-Louise. "Ikat Weaving from Southern Europe." *Palette,* no. 30 (1968): 2-13.

Exhibition Staff

Alan Shestack, *Director*
Timothy Fiske, *Associate Director*
Michael Conforti, *Chairman, Curatorial Division; Bell Memorial Curator of Decorative Arts and Sculpture*
Lotus Stack, *Curator of Textiles; curator in charge of exhibition*
Mary Ann Butterfield, *Assistant Curator, Textiles*
Peggy Dorwick, *Administrative Assistant, Textiles*
Robert Jacobsen, *Curator, Asian Art*
Catherine Parker, *Curatorial Assistant, Asian Art*
Mary Mancuso, *Exhibitions Coordinator*
Kathryn Johnson, *Chairman, Education Division*
Mary Huber, *Supervisor, Visitor Services*
Gary Mortensen, *Photographer*
Robert Fogt, *Photographic Technician*
Louise Lincoln, *Editor*
Elisabeth Sövik, *Associate Editor*
Ruth Dean, *Designer*
Anne Knauff, *Assistant Designer*
R. Patrick Atherton, *Typesetter*
Liz Sela, *Director of Public Relations*
Alla Litkewitsch, *Administrative Assistant, Public Relations*
Kathy Hedberg, *Public Relations Assistant*
Laura Johnson, *Scheduling Coordinator*
Gwen Bitz, *Registrar*
Karen Duncan, *Associate Registrar*
Claire Ouellette, *Assistant Registrar*
Shawn Spurgin, *Registration Assistant*
Roxy Ballard, *Exhibition Designer*
John Black, *Lighting Technician*
Susan Wood, *Collection Maintenance Technician*
Ken Krenz, *Storage Technician*
Nina Chenault, Tom Jance, Doug Kroeger, Patti Landres, Theo Manzavrakos, Wayne Masterson, Brian Stieler, Gregg Zimmer, *Exhibitions Technicians*
Jan Blanchard, *Maintenance Supervisor*
Gordon Cable, *Chief of Security*